May 21–June 21

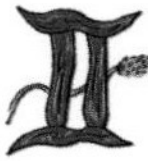

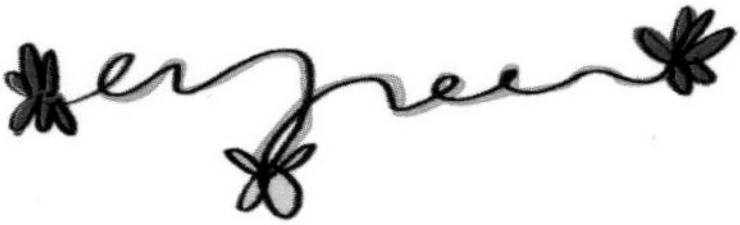

Liberty Phi

GEMINI

INTRODUCTION

Astrology is all about the planets in our skies and what energy and characteristics influence us. From ancient times, people have wanted to understand the rhythms of life and looked to the skies and their celestial bodies for inspiration, and the ancient constellations are there in the 12 zodiac signs we recognise from astrology. The Ancient Greeks devised narratives related to myths and legends about their celestial ancestors, to which they referred to make decisions and choices. Roman mythology did the same and over the years these ancient wisdoms became refined into today's modern astrology.

The configuration of the planets in the sky at the time and place of our birth is unique to each and every one of us, and what this means and how it plays out throughout our lives is both fascinating and informative. Just knowing which planet rules your sun sign is the beginning of an exploratory journey that can provide you with a useful tool for life.

Understanding the meaning, energetic nature and power of each planet, where this sits in your birth chart and what this might mean is all important information and linked to your date, place and time of birth, relevant *only* to you. Completely individual, the way in which you can work with the power of the planets comes from understanding their qualities and how this might influence the position in which they sit in your chart.

What knowledge of astrology can give you is the tools for working out how a planetary pattern might influence you, because of its relationship to your particular planetary configuration and circumstances. Each sun sign has a set of characteristics linked to its ruling planet – for example, Gemini is ruled by Mercury – and, in turn, to each of the 12 Houses (see page 81) that form the structure of every individual's birth chart (see page 78). Once you know the meanings of these and how these relate to different areas of your life, you can begin to work out what might be relevant to you when, for example, you read in a magazine horoscope that there's a Full Moon in Capricorn or that Jupiter is transiting Mars.

Each of the 12 astrological or zodiac sun signs is ruled by a planet (see page 52) and looking at a planet's characteristics will give you an indication of the influences brought to bear on each sign. It's useful to have a general understanding of these influences, because your birth chart includes many of them, in different house or planetary configurations, which gives you information about how uniquely *you* you are. Also included in this book are the minor planets (see page 102), also relevant to the information your chart provides.

GEMINI

Our sun sign is determined by the date of our birth wherever we are born, and if you are a Gemini you were born between May 21st and June 21st. Bear in mind, however, that if you were born on one or other of those actual dates it's worth checking your *time* of birth, if you know it, against the year you were born and where. That's because no one is born 'on the cusp' (see page 78) and because there will be a moment on those days when Taurus shifts to Gemini, and Gemini shifts to Cancer. It's well worth a check, especially if you've never felt quite convinced that the characteristics of your designated sun sign match your own.

The constellation of Gemini is formed by 17 stars, including the bright star Pollux and the less bright star Castor. Although they were twins and the sons of Leda in Greek mythology, they had different fathers. Pollux's father was a god, which made him immortal, while Castor's father was mortal. But when the twins died, Zeus made Castor immortal so that they could be together forever in the night sky.

Gemini is ruled by Mercury, the messenger of the gods able to move swiftly through the skies thanks to his winged heels, so this sign is gifted with a bright, intellectually sharp ability to communicate at speed and with wit.

An air sign (like Aquarius and Libra), Gemini has the airiness of flight, and can be rather flighty as a consequence, with something of a butterfly brain, able to flit from one topic to another, requiring the need to learn to focus without distraction. Gemini is also a mutable sign (like Virgo, Sagittarius and Pisces), well able to adapt to new situations and respond to new ideas and people, and is mentally very adept at being able to spot and process new information. While Gemini is able to harness their thoughts at speed, they're not necessarily the most thoughtful or considerate of the sun signs. With a tendency to flit quickly from one situation to the next, they can sometimes forget that others may need a little more time to catch up.

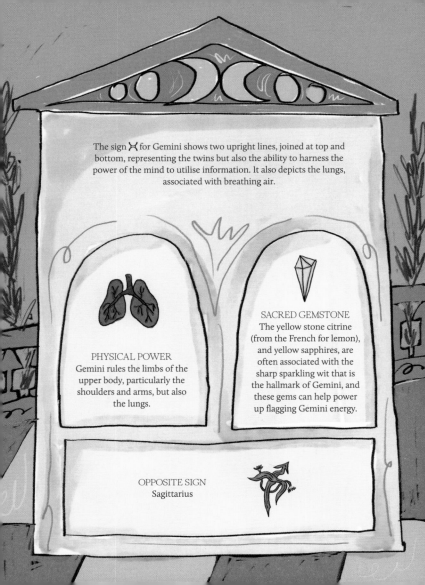

The sign ♊ for Gemini shows two upright lines, joined at top and bottom, representing the twins but also the ability to harness the power of the mind to utilise information. It also depicts the lungs, associated with breathing air.

PHYSICAL POWER
Gemini rules the limbs of the upper body, particularly the shoulders and arms, but also the lungs.

SACRED GEMSTONE
The yellow stone citrine (from the French for lemon), and yellow sapphires, are often associated with the sharp sparkling wit that is the hallmark of Gemini, and these gems can help power up flagging Gemini energy.

OPPOSITE SIGN
Sagittarius

Gemini is depicted by the twins and this sun sign also has something of a duality about it, a restless energy that is both curious and communicative. So not only does Gemini want to know all about what's happening, they want to tell everyone they meet about it too.

Ruled by the god of communication, Mercury, this characteristic lies at the heart of Gemini, who love to communicate in a variety of ways and their smartphone is often in regular use. Texting, emailing, Googling, Facetime and WhatsApp, their phone is seldom far from their hand and they love to express themselves across their multiple social media accounts too. All this online activity can make Gemini seem rather hyperactive and distracted, and while it's true they can get a lot done, they may need to learn to put their phone aside occasionally and engage one-to-one with

♓

others in real life. Otherwise they can get a bit of a reputation for superficiality.

Travel is another attraction for Gemini, and some may happily choose to put down roots in several places over the course of their lives, because they love variety and new experiences and are unafraid of cutting loose and starting over. This may be because they change jobs and locations, working for a global company that appoints them as regional heads. Or they may opt for a freelance life in some line of media, allowing them to work out of a remote location, thanks to internet connectivity.

Holidays are often spent in far-flung places too, because new locations automatically promise new people and experiences, towards which Gemini quite naturally gravitates.

This tendency to find new locations and experiences attractive isn't limited to youthful Geminis either. Post-retirement may find many of them upping sticks and rejuvenating their outlook through travel. Curiosity is a great instigator and this is what keeps many Geminis young at heart. And that's another striking feature because Gemini often retains a very youthful energy and fit physique and looks much younger than their years.

For Gemini, their public face is very closely aligned to their private face. Not for them the murkier reaches of emotional depths, their emotions are generally well expressed and their lover, friends, family and work colleagues tend to find them easy to understand. What's also interesting is the diversity of Gemini's friends and work colleagues. Because they are so well able to communicate, they find it easy to adapt their persona to those of others. While Gemini may have to learn patience with those who are not so quick on the uptake, they can be so charmingly adamant about their own point of view that others are willing to accept their occasionally sharp-edged tongue.

THE MOON IN
YOUR CHART

W hile your zodiac sign is your sun sign, making you a
sun sign Gemini, the Moon also plays a role in your
birth chart and if you know the time and place of your
birth, along with your birth date, you can get your birth chart done
(see page 78). From this you can discover in which zodiac sign your
Moon is positioned in your chart.

The Moon reflects the characteristics of who you are at the time
of your birth, your innate personality, how you express yourself and
how you are seen by others. This is in contrast to our sun sign which
indicates the more dominant characteristics we reveal as we travel
through life. The Moon also represents the feminine in our natal
chart (the Sun the masculine) and the sign in which our Moon falls
can indicate how we express the feminine side of our personality.
Looking at the two signs together in our charts immediately creates
a balance.

MOON IN GEMINI

The Moon spends roughly 2.5 days in each zodiac sign as it moves through all 12 signs during its monthly cycle. This means that the Moon is regularly in Gemini, and it can be useful to know when this occurs and in particular when we have a New Moon or a Full Moon in Gemini because these are especially good times for you to focus your energy and intentions.

A New Moon is always the start of a new cycle, an opportunity to set new intentions for the coming month, and when this is in your own sign, Gemini, you can benefit from this additional energy and support. The Full Moon is an opportunity to reflect on the culmination of your earlier intentions.

NEW MOON
IN GEMINI AFFIRMATION

'I will lighten my heart and make new connections,
powering up my communication skills to realise my
hopes and dreams at the start of this new cycle.'

FULL MOON
IN GEMINI AFFIRMATION

'In the Full Moon's reflected light I use my breath
to energise my focus as I inhale life in
to strengthen my purpose and resolve,
remembering to keep grounded.'

GEMINI HEALTH

Gemini rules the upper limbs, the shoulders and arms in particular, but also the lungs through which air enters and leaves the body. Shoulder muscles can grow tense from excessive hours spent on the computer, and also repetitive strain injury in the arms. Keeping strong and supple and avoiding overuse of the upper limbs will help prevent chronic problems. Some Geminis might also be affected by lung problems, perhaps asthma, either in childhood which they grow out of, or later in life. Also, breathing exercises can be a useful way of learning to calm down an over-excited sympathetic nervous system, which will help with any tendency towards anxiety that might arise.

Gemini has a naturally active disposition and doesn't tend to become overweight, but there may be issues around strength and suppleness, especially in the arms and shoulders, and muscle tension radiating up into the neck. Unlikely to stick at any one form of exercise for long, Gemini tends to get bored of the routine of the gym or Pilates class. Cross-country running may appeal as it gets fresh air into the lungs, while swimming will do wonders for weak arms and shoulders. The main problem though is sticking with it, and it may take some serious injury or affliction to help Gemini see the wisdom of maintaining their health consistently rather than in fits and starts.

POWER UP
YOUR GEMINI
ENERGY

There are often moments or periods when we feel uninspired, demotivated and low in energy. At these times it's worth working with your innate sun sign energy to power up again, and paying attention to what Gemini relishes and needs can help support both physical and mental health.

Fresh air is always balm to a Gemini's soul, especially on sunny days when just being outdoors can lift their mood, and this can be just the inspiration needed to help re-energise body and mind. What's also useful is to ground some of that dissipated airiness, to harness this energy through connection with the earth. Just feeling the earth beneath our feet, particularly by walking barefoot when we can, goes a long way to reconnect us to our physical and emotional roots.

Although not particularly prone to depression or anxiety, like everyone Gemini can reach the point of exhaustion or become overwhelmed from burning the candle at both ends or pushing hard to reach a deadline. At this point it's important to recognise potential or actual burnout and take steps to avoid its worst impact. Sleep can become elusive to hyperactive airheads and calming the body can help calm the mind. At this point some hands-on massage therapy can help reconnect the body to the mind, reducing tension in the muscles while also stimulating the hormone oxytocin to help soothe the nervous system and facilitate restful sleep.

A nutritious diet is important to busy Gemini, who may find themselves so distracted they literally forget to eat, or endlessly rely on energy snacks rather than balanced nutrition to support their hectic lifestyle. A variety of flavours and textures is always going to be important to pique their appetite, and many love soufflés, mousses and meringues, where the egg whites give the dish an airy lift. Leafy green vegetables, along with avocados, bananas, nuts and seeds and lentils, will provide magnesium, a mineral that has a calming effect on muscle tissue and also aids sleep, which the occasionally hyperactive Gemini will benefit from.

When it comes to herbs, parsley is also high in magnesium and good for Gemini, along with lemongrass and marjoram, while root spices like ginger and liquorice, and spices like cardamom and cinnamon, can help stimulate a fickle appetite.

Utilise a New Moon in Gemini with a ritual to set your intentions and power up: light a candle, use essential oil of rose to stimulate your mood and concentration (this oil blends well with grounding cardamom and inspiring vetiver), focus your thoughts on the change you wish to see and allow time to meditate on this. Place your gemstone (see page 13) in the moonlight. Write down your intentions and keep in a safe place. Meditate on the New Moon in Gemini affirmation (see page 21).

At a Full Moon in Gemini you will have the benefit of the Sun's reflected light to help illuminate what is working for you and what you can let go, because the Full Moon brings clarity. Focus on this with another ritual, taking the time to meditate on the Full Moon in Gemini affirmation (see page 21). Light a candle, place your gemstone in the moonlight and make a note of your thoughts and feelings, strengthened by the Moon in your sign.

GEMINI'S SPIRITUAL HOME

K nowing where to go to replenish your soul and recharge your batteries both physically and spiritually is important and worth serious consideration. Many Geminis gravitate towards city living, because they love a social vibe and meeting people, and get a real kick out of diversity, which can mean their spiritual home is actually a location far from where they were born.

Wherever they hail from, there are also a number of countries that particularly resonate with airy Gemini energy, including Morocco, Iceland, Sweden and Eritrea. Alternate lifestyles and cultures create no boundaries for Geminis, who love to explore new ideas and attitudes, open-mindedly engaging in the sights, sounds and landscapes new horizons offer.

Even holiday destinations have to offer a bit of this. From partying on a Thai beach with strangers to admiring the legacy of the ancient Greeks at the Acropolis, energy and activity are very much Gemini's way of recharging their spiritual batteries.

G E M

W O M A N

I N I

This woman is one of the most responsive of the sun signs. Her response might vary from the sublime to the ridiculous, but this is not someone for whom the cold shoulder is a valid form of communication. She has to let you know what she's thinking, whether it's good, bad or indifferent, because planet Mercury has gifted her the art of communication. But, like Mercury, she's constantly on the move and if she finds the company boring, she soon moves on to the next new thing or person.

The downside of this apparent flippancy is that she doesn't always get taken seriously as a contender, whether at work or in her relationships. It's hard to invest in someone emotionally if they appear to be constantly looking over your shoulder for the next thing to spark their interest. But this quick-fire interest and curiosity is part of the charm for which many Gemini women are renowned; the focus of their attention (however brief this might be) is utterly beguiled and made to feel like the only one on the planet that matters to her, which at that moment is true.

In appearance she is often amazingly dressed, with a completely individual way of putting her look together, mixing vintage, high street or couture together with originality. Gemini likes to express themselves through what they wear and 'dressing the part' often comes completely naturally to this woman.

Her friends and lovers may not have much in common with each other, because what she often looks for in others are those characteristics that appeal to her own Gemini duality. A party hosted by a Gemini is often one of the most interesting; because their range of friends, work colleagues and lovers is so diverse, they will either click or clash together when they meet.

For all this, she can be hard to read and come across as rather fickle, but at heart there's a perceptive and responsive friend or lover who, given half the chance, will reward efforts at a relationship with real commitment. It can feel as if Gemini woman has to test out her lovers and friendships to feel secure, because that airy free spirit does need a little grounding and security to feel loved, and to love in return.

G E M

M

A

N

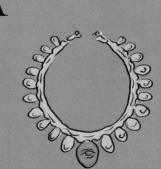

I N I

With an easy sociability, this man tends to radiate wit and charm, and is seldom short of company, whether it's a casual exchange with a stranger in a bar or a hot date for a friend's wedding. Happy to engage with all and sundry, Gemini attracts everyone from the baby in the buggy to the elderly person who needs help crossing the road. This is a man who actively likes to connect and is open to all sorts of encounters, thanks to the curiosity gifted him by planet Mercury. And it's completely genuine. The only off-note is that once his interest peaks, he has a tendency to immediately shift his focus elsewhere. All of which can give him the reputation for being rather fickle in his attention, which is not completely true, he just tends to blow hot and cold in response to what's happening around him.

There's an airy approach to much of life for Gemini, which can sometimes give the impression of superficiality. But this can arise from an attempt to keep the general mood light at home or at work, or when with lovers, friends

and work colleagues, because Gemini can find too much emotion difficult and may shy away from it, masking any discomfort with what can come across as flippancy. As he matures, most Geminis become more comfortable with other people's emotions, no longer feeling responsible for them, which avoids misunderstandings and makes it easier for everyone to connect and communicate, which is his preferred outcome.

As a friend, Gemini loves to intellectually analyse problems, and is often fascinated by other people's, which can make him an excellent companion for anyone needing to talk through a difficult situation. He's often happier with other people's emotions when they are one step removed, and is capable of offering real insight because he is not engaged emotionally. This is one way he shows he cares, by offering a friend or lover the commitment of an intelligent, thoughtful response. And they do tend to look on the bright side, which can also be enormously helpful when times are tricky.

GEMINI IN LOVE

Partly because of the duality of this sun sign, sometimes it's not easy to tell if Gemini is in love or not because they don't always communicate the more obvious signs of romance, often shying away initially from emotional declarations. In fact, Gemini may play it rather cool at the beginning of a relationship – responsive, yes, but not quite engaged, almost as if they are hedging their bets. But this cautious display is just the other side of intensity, and they are capable of flipping from one to the other, which can be disconcerting for the person in receipt of their love. Truth is, Gemini tends to focus on one thing at a time, and in between focusing on the one they love, they can appear quite disengaged and preoccupied with something else.

GEMINI AS
A LOVER

Gemini in love is looking for their soulmate, a spiritual twin who will match and mirror themselves. Opposites do attract, but given the duality of Gemini's nature, they are often attracted to something they recognise at an unconscious level, so it's not always obvious, even to themselves, why they are attracted to someone.

Sexual attraction is very much to do with the mind as much as physical appearance. Being able to communicate with a lover ranks high on Gemini's list of priorities. An evening spent with Gemini can often feel a bit like an intellectual rather than a romantic exercise, as they will probably want to know what their date thinks about politics, a recent bestselling novel, the latest must-see TV series or even the day's weather. Woe betide their lover if they don't have an opinion. This can make dating a Gemini rather an intense affair. Although they do relax eventually on a date, it can sometimes take a while.

But because seduction is a lovely game, Geminis actually take a light-hearted approach to dating in spite of this rigorous questioning. In fact, the shift from conversation to consummation can be so subtle, a lover may be taken by surprise. For them, dating can be all about trying out different types of relationships and Gemini often surprises their family and friends with the diversity of their lovers. The same approach applies to sex: experimentation is often part of the package when it comes to Gemini. Many Geminis make adventurous lovers and thrive on variety, although this can sometimes mean various partners at the same time. They tend to respond happily to many different types of people and want to be free to explore before they settle down and finally commit to their soulmate.

WHAT'S IN GEMINI'S BEDSIDE CABINET?

The love poetry of Pablo Neruda

Sex dice to keep the ideas coming

Gently restraining handcuffs to keep them focused

WHICH SIGN SUITS GEMINI?

In relationships with Gemini, the sun sign of the other person and the ruling planet of that sign can bring out the best, or sometimes the worst, in a lover. Knowing what might spark, smoulder or suffocate love is worth closer investigation, but always remember that sun sign astrology is only a starting point for any relationship.

GEMINI
AND ARIES

There's much to stimulate this relationship, with Mars and Mercury bringing action and communication to the fore, so there's already a mutual attraction. If this can weather any initial tempestuousness, it's a good match.

GEMINI
AND TAURUS

Taurus' Venus brings a gentle, grounding harmony to Gemini's occasionally wilful airiness, and as long as they can manage to communicate their differences, what they do have in common can create the basis for an enduring love affair.

GEMINI
AND GEMINI

This could be a perfect match or a perfect disaster depending on whether they can manage to accommodate each other's duality, but being equally communicative may be just the intellectual stimulation they each need for a lasting relationship.

GEMINI
AND CANCER

Gentle, home-loving Cancer may find Mercury's constant dance around their moon exhausting after a while, but Gemini often responds well to being nurtured, creating the possibility of a relationship from which both can benefit equally.

GEMINI
AND LEO

While Gemini might find Leo's capacity for constant exuberance difficult to accommodate, the lion might find Mercury's constant requirement to discuss everything annoying when the lion's Sun just wants to shine without interruption.

GEMINI
AND VIRGO

Both are ruled by planet Mercury and both are mutable sun signs, while Virgo's earthiness can help ground Gemini's airy nature. So as long as they allow each other room for manoeuvre, this match can be surprisingly harmonious.

GEMINI
AND LIBRA

Two air signs, they speak the same
initial language, and Libra's desire
for balance can suit Gemini's duality,
although Libra's Venus influence can
sometimes find Mercury irritatingly
superficial, which can cause
arguments.

GEMINI AND
SCORPIO

Although Gemini is often highly
intrigued and fascinated by Scorpio's
Pluto aspects, over time this might
dampen the spirits of even the most
airy of signs, so there's a deep need for
understanding and often compromise
for this partnership to work.

GEMINI AND
SAGITTARIUS

Both like to explore and travel in body
and mind, which creates a strong
initial attraction. Sagittarius' jovial
Jupiter characteristics often suit
Gemini's mercurial spark, so this can
be a strong and lasting relationship.

GEMINI AND CAPRICORN

Capricorn's Saturn can often be rather hard on Gemini's mercurial approach to life, sometimes trying to bring them to heel. But if they can accommodate each other's differences, there's often a good, beneficial bond between this earth and air sign.

GEMINI AND AQUARIUS

Both air signs, Gemini can sometimes become frustrated by Aquarius' unpredictable and humanitarian take on life, thanks to ruling planet Uranus, and unless this is overcome it tends to make communication tricky between the two.

GEMINI AND PISCES

Gemini's quick-witted take on life can find Pisces' dreamy Neptune influence too slow, but if they can establish communication, they fascinate each other and this initial attraction can grow into a long-lasting bond.

GEMINI AT
WORK

Generally, anything to do with communication will appeal to Gemini as a career or place of work, whether this is as a newspaper journalist or IT engineer. Whatever they choose to do, and Gemini may change careers several times, it is likely to involve communication of ideas or information in one form or another.

Although they're inclined to be sociable, Geminis tend to be equally happy working in a team or alone. In a team they tend to be somewhat unpredictable, something of a maverick who comes up with original approaches to problem-solving. But while they can be good at deadlines, Gemini often skids in at the eleventh hour which can make other team members nervous. Luckily their responsiveness and charm can ease difficulties with all but the most conformist of workmates, but it may not do much for their boss's blood pressure. Which is why Geminis often prefer to be the boss, maybe in an entrepreneurial start-up, or to work alone as a freelancer, keeping their own hours and setting their own deadlines.

Intellectual stimulation is key for Gemini. This might find them drawn to the sort of application to detail required by the legal profession, which, if they choose the right strand to appeal to their social nature, like entertainment law, might suit perfectly. Researching and writing is often attractive to Gemini, but it has to be in an area that is of continuing interest. A career in theatre, where playing a different part and communicating it, acting in its broadest sense, attracts many Geminis. And those professions that require a degree of performance in communication, like being a barrister, teacher or lecturer, can also attract.

Remuneration is often not much of a driver for Gemini; maintaining interest at work is more of a priority. This can find them changing jobs or moving locations every few years. And although they are often financially successful because of their ability to burn the midnight oil when necessary, Geminis can also have the knack of identifying and monetising future trends in some way. This has particularly been the case with the development of internet technologies and app development, which often fascinates those born under the influence of planet Mercury.

GEMINI
AT HOME

Home as a concept isn't as important to Gemini as to other signs, and they may move a lot in their lifetime, even across countries and continents. What's interesting though is that as an air sign many Geminis will gravitate towards homes with lots of light and air, and often an open-plan spaciousness to achieve this. There's unlikely to be much clutter either, although some Geminis will have a lot of books on shelves and in piles by their bed. But high-speed connectivity for their internet is often a first priority for those ruled by the planet Mercury, along with all the latest devices to access it. They cannot bear to be disconnected from the world and their smart phone is unlikely ever to be completely turned off.

Geminis tend not to look back but are generally in forward motion, so their home is unlikely to contain many relics of their ancestors or past. They may have a few family photos tucked away, but heirlooms hold little attraction. For Gemini, their home is a place to socialise as much as to rest, and to party. Many Geminis are party animals and particularly enjoy impromptu informal gatherings of everyone they know, while often expressing the view that a friend is a stranger you've not yet met. Which can make living with Gemini an unpredictable affair, as they arrive home with six guests for dinner and have their favourite takeaway restaurant on speed dial. Or they are capable of responding immediately to an idea on a whim, whether this is to repaint the kitchen overnight, up-sticks and move across the country, or invite someone to stay for a month. And this is where their communication skills can go awry, as it may not occur to them to consult the rest of the household.

FREE THE
SPIRIT

U nderstanding your own sun sign astrology is only part of
the picture. It provides you with a template to examine and
reflect on your own life's journey but also the context for
this through your relationships with others, intimate or otherwise,
and within the culture and environment in which you live.

Throughout time, the Sun and planets of our universe have
kept to their paths and astrologers have used this ancient wisdom
to understand the pattern of the universe. In this way, astrology is
a tool to utilise these wisdoms, a way of helping make sense of the
energies we experience as the planets shift in our skies.

'A physician without a knowledge of astrology has no right to
call himself a physician,' said Hippocrates, the Greek physician born
in 460 BC, who understood better than anyone how these psychic
energies worked. As did Carl Jung, the 20th-century philosopher and
psychoanalyst, because he said, 'Astrology represents the summation
of all the psychological knowledge of antiquity.'

THE 10
PLANETS

SUN

Although the Sun is officially a star, for the purpose of astrology it's considered a planet. It is also the centre of our universe and gives us both light and energy; our lives are dependent on it and it embodies our creative life force. As a life giver, the Sun is considered a masculine entity, the patriarch and ruler of the skies. Our sun sign is where we start our astrological journey whichever sign it falls in, and as long as we know which day of which month we were born, we have this primary knowledge.

MOON

We now know that the Moon is actually a natural satellite of the Earth (the third planet from the Sun) rather than a planet but is considered such for the purposes of astrology. It's dependent on the Sun for its reflected light, and it is only through their celestial relationship that we can see it. In this way, the Moon in each of our birth charts depicts the feminine energy to balance the masculine Sun's life force, the ying to its yang. It is not an impotent or subservient presence, particularly when you consider how it gives the world's oceans their tides, the relentless energy of the ebb and flow powering up the seas. The Moon's energy also helps illuminate our unconscious desires, helping to bring these to the service of our self-knowledge.

MERCURY

Mercury, messenger of the gods, has always been associated with speed and agility, whether in body or mind. Because of this, Mercury is considered to be the planet of quick wit and anything requiring verbal dexterity and the application of intelligence. Those with Mercury prominent in their chart love exchanging and debating ideas and telling stories (often with a tendency to embellish the truth of a situation), making them prominent in professions where these qualities are valuable.

Astronomically, Mercury is the closest planet to the Sun and moves around a lot in our skies. What's also relevant is that several times a year Mercury appears to be retrograde (see page 99) which has the effect of slowing down or disrupting its influence.

VENUS

The goddess of beauty, love and pleasure. Venus is the second planet from the Sun and benefits from this proximity, having received its positive vibes. Depending on which astrological sign Venus falls in your chart will influence how you relate to art and culture and the opposite sex. The characteristics of this sign will tell you all you need to know about what you aspire to, where you seek and how you experience pleasure, along with the types of lover you attract. Again, partly depending on where it's placed, Venus can sometimes increase self-indulgence which can be a less positive aspect of a hedonistic life.

MARS

RULES THE ASTROLOGICAL SIGN OF ARIES

This big, powerful planet is fourth from the Sun and exerts an energetic force, powering up the characteristics of the astrological sign in which it falls in your chart. This will tell you how you assert yourself, whether your anger flares or smoulders, what might stir your passion and how you express your sexual desires. Mars will show you what works best for you to turn ideas into action, the sort of energy you might need to see something through and how your independent spirit can be most effectively engaged.

JUPITER

Big, bountiful Jupiter is the largest planet in our solar
system and fifth from the Sun. It heralds optimism,
generosity and general benevolence. Whichever sign
Jupiter falls in in your chart is where you will find
the characteristics for your particular experience of
luck, happiness and good fortune. Jupiter will show
you which areas to focus on to gain the most and
best from your life. Wherever Jupiter appears in your
chart it will bring a positive influence and when it's
prominent in our skies we all benefit.

SATURN

RULES THE ASTROLOGICAL SIGN OF CAPRICORN

Saturn is considered akin to Old Father Time, with all the patience, realism and wisdom that archetype evokes. Sometimes called the taskmaster of the skies, its influence is all about how we handle responsibility and it requires that we graft and apply ourselves in order to learn life's lessons. The sixth planet from the Sun, Saturn's 'return' (see page 100) to its place in an individual's birth chart occurs approximately every 28 years. How self-disciplined you are about overcoming opposition or adversity will be influenced by the characteristics of the sign in which this powerful planet falls in your chart.

URANUS

The seventh planet from the Sun, Uranus is the planet of unpredictability, change and surprise, and whether you love or loathe the impact of Uranus will depend in part on which astrological sign it influences in your chart. How you respond to its influence is entirely up to the characteristics of the sign it occupies in your chart. Whether you see the change it heralds as a gift or a curse is up to you, but because it takes seven years to travel through a sign, its presence in a sign can influence a generation.

NEPTUNE

Neptune ruled the sea, and this planet is all about deep waters of mystery, imagination and secrets. It's also representative of our spiritual side so the characteristics of whichever astrological sign it occupies in your chart will influence how this plays out in your life. Neptune is the eighth planet from the Sun and its influence can be subtle and mysterious. The astrological sign in which it falls in your chart will indicate how you realise your vision, dream and goals. The only precaution is if it falls in an equally watery sign, creating a potential difficulty in distinguishing between fantasy and reality.

PLUTO

Pluto is the furthest planet from the Sun and exerts a regenerative energy that transforms but often requires destruction to erase what's come before in order to begin again. Its energy often lies dormant and then erupts, so the astrological sign in which it falls will have a bearing on how this might play out in your chart. Transformation can be very positive but also very painful. When Pluto's influence is strong, change occurs and how you react or respond to this will be very individual. Don't fear it, but reflect on how to use its energy to your benefit.

YOUR SUN SIGN

Your sun or zodiac sign is the one in which you were born, determined by the date of your birth. Your sun sign is ruled by a specific planet. For example, Gemini is ruled by Mercury but Capricorn by Saturn, so we already have the first piece of information and the first piece of our individual jigsaw puzzle.

The next piece of the jigsaw is understanding that the energy of a particular planet in your birth chart (see page 78) plays out via the characteristics of the astrological sign in which it's positioned, and this is hugely valuable in understanding some of the patterns of your life. You may have your Sun in Gemini, and a good insight into the characteristics of this sign, but what if you have Neptune in Leo? Or Venus in Aries? Uranus in Virgo? Understanding the impact of these influences can help you reflect on the way you react or respond and the choices you can make, helping to ensure more positive outcomes.

If, for example, with Uranus in Taurus you are resistant to change, remind yourself that change is inevitable and can be positive, allowing you to work with it rather than against its influence. If you have Neptune in Virgo, it will bring a more spiritual element to this practical earth sign, while Mercury in Aquarius will enhance the predictive element of your analysis and judgement. The scope and range and useful aspect of having this knowledge is just the beginning of how you can utilise astrology to live your best life.

In addition, the planets do not stay still. They are said to transit (move) through the course of an astrological year. Those closest to us, like Mercury, transit quite regularly (every 88 days), while those further away, like Pluto, take much longer, in this case 248 years to come full circle. So the effects of each planet can vary depending on their position and this is why we hear astrologers talk about someone's Saturn return (see page 100), Mercury retrograde (see page 99) or about Capricorn (or other sun sign) 'weather'. This is indicative of an influence that can be anticipated and worked with and is both universal and personal. The shifting positions of the planets bring an influence to bear on each of us, linked to the position of our own planetary influences and how these have a bearing on each other. If you understand the nature of these planetary influences you can begin to work with, rather than against, them and this information can be very much to your benefit.

First, though, you need to take a look at the component parts of astrology, the pieces of your personal jigsaw, then you'll have the information you need to make sense of how your sun sign might be affected during the changing patterns of the planets.

YOUR BIRTH CHART

With the date, time and place of birth, you can easily find out where your (or anyone else's) planets are positioned from an online astrological chart programme (see page 110). This will give you an exact sun sign position, which you probably already know, but it can also be useful if you think you were born 'on the cusp' because it will give you an *exact* indication of what sign you were born in. In addition, this natal chart will tell you your Ascendant sign, which sign your Moon is in, along with the other planets specific to your personal and completely individual chart and the Houses (see page 81) in which the astrological signs are positioned.

A birth chart is divided into 12 sections, representing each of the 12 Houses (see pages 82–85) with your Ascendant or Rising sign always positioned in the 1st House, and the other 11 Houses running counter-clockwise from one to 12.

ASCENDANT OR RISING SIGN

Your Ascendant is a first, important part of the complexity of an individual birth chart. While your sun sign gives you an indication of the personality you will inhabit through the course of your life, it is your Ascendant or Rising sign – which is the sign rising at the break of dawn on the Eastern horizon at the time and on the date of your birth – that often gives a truer indication of how you will project your personality and consequently how the world sees you. So even though you were born a sun sign Gemini, whatever sign your Ascendant is in, for example Cancer, will be read through the characteristics of this astrological sign.

Your Ascendant is always in your 1st House, which is the House of the Self (see page 82) and the other houses always follow the same consecutive astrological order. So if, for example, your Ascendant is Leo, then your second house is in Virgo, your third house in Libra, and so on. Each house has its own characteristics but how these will play out in your individual chart will be influenced by the sign positioned in it.

Opposite your Ascendant is your Descendant sign, positioned in the 7th House (see page 84) and this shows what you look for in a partnership, your complementary 'other half' as it were. There's always something intriguing about what the Descendant can help us to understand, and it's worth knowing yours and being on the lookout for it when considering a long-term marital or business partnership.

THE
12
HOUSES

While each of the 12 Houses represent different aspects of our lives, they are also ruled by one of the 12 astrological signs, giving each house its specific characteristics. When we discover, for example, that we have Capricorn in the 12th House, this might suggest a pragmatic or practical approach to spirituality. Or, if you had Gemini in your 6th House, this might suggest a rather airy approach to organisation.

1ST HOUSE

RULED BY ARIES

The first impression you give walking into
a room, how you like to be seen, your sense
of self and the energy with which you
approach life.

2ND HOUSE

RULED BY TAURUS

What you value, including what you own
that provides your material security; your
self-value and work ethic, how you earn
your income.

3RD HOUSE

RULED BY GEMINI

How you communicate through words,
deeds and gestures; also how you learn and
function in a group, including within your
own family.

4 TH HOUSE

RULED BY CANCER

This is about your home, your security
and how you take care of yourself and
your family; and also about those family
traditions you hold dear.

5 TH HOUSE

RULED BY LEO

Creativity in all its forms, including fun
and eroticism, intimate relationships and
procreation, self-expression
and positive fulfilment.

6 TH HOUSE

RULED BY VIRGO

How you organise your daily routine, your
health, your business affairs, and how you
are of service to others, from those
in your family to the workplace.

7TH HOUSE

RULED BY LIBRA

This is about partnerships and shared
goals, whether marital or in business, and
what we look for in these to complement
ourselves.

8TH HOUSE

RULED BY SCORPIO

Regeneration, through death and rebirth,
and also our legacy and how this might
be realised through sex, procreation and
progeny.

9TH HOUSE

RULED BY SAGITTARIUS

Our world view, cultures outside our
own and the bigger picture beyond our
immediate horizon, to which we travel
either in body or mind.

10TH HOUSE

RULED BY CAPRICORN

Our aims and ambitions in life, what we aspire to and what we're prepared to do to achieve it; this is how we approach our working lives.

11TH HOUSE

RULED BY AQUARIUS

The house of humanity and our friendships, our relationships with the wider world, our tribe or group to which we feel an affiliation.

12TH HOUSE

RULED BY PISCES

Our spiritual side resides here. Whether this is religious or not, it embodies our inner life, beliefs and the deeper connections we forge.

THE FOUR ELEMENTS

The 12 astrological signs are divided into four groups, representing the four elements: fire, water, earth and air. This gives each of the three signs in each group additional characteristics.

FIRE

ARIES ⚭ LEO ⚭ SAGITTARIUS

Embodying warmth, spontaneity and enthusiasm.

WATER

CANCER ❧ SCORPIO ❧ PISCES

Embodying a more feeling, spiritual and intuitive side.

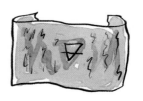

EARTH

TAURUS ❧ VIRGO ❧ CAPRICORN

Grounded and sure-footed and sometimes rather stubborn.

♓   GEMINI

AIR

GEMINI ❧ LIBRA ❧ AQUARIUS

Flourishing in the world of vision, ideas and perception.

FIXED,
CARDINAL OR
MUTABLE?

The 12 signs are further divided into three groups of four, giving additional characteristics of being fixed, cardinal or mutable. These represent the way in which they respond to situations.

FIXED

TAURUS, LEO, SCORPIO AND AQUARIUS
ARE FIXED SIGNS

Their energy tends to be steady and they are less
reactive, more responsive, although they can have
a tendency to be resistant to change and need
encouragement.

CARDINAL

ARIES, CANCER, LIBRA AND
CAPRICORN ARE CARDINAL SIGNS

Their energy is often instinctive and action-oriented,
enabling them to get things started, although there's
sometimes a tendency to fail to carry things through.

MUTABLE

GEMINI, VIRGO, SAGITTARIUS AND
PISCES ARE MUTABLE SIGNS

The clue here is their adaptability and responsiveness to
change, which they don't fear, and readiness to listen to
and embrace new ideas.

MERCURY RETROGRADE

This occurs several times over the astrological year and lasts for around four weeks, with a shadow week either side (a quick Google search will tell you the forthcoming dates). It's important what sign Mercury is in while it's retrograde, because its impact will be affected by the characteristics of that sign. For example, if Mercury is retrograde in Gemini, the sign of communication that is ruled by Mercury, the effect will be keenly felt in all areas of communication. However, if Mercury is retrograde in Aquarius, which rules the house of friendships and relationships, this may keenly affect our communication with large groups, or if in Sagittarius, which rules the house of travel, it could affect travel itineraries and encourage us to check our documents carefully.

Mercury retrograde can also be seen as an opportunity to pause, review or reconsider ideas and plans, to regroup, recalibrate and recuperate, and generally to take stock of where we are and how we might proceed. In our fast-paced 24/7 lives, Mercury retrograde can often be a useful opportunity to slow down and allow ourselves space to restore some necessary equilibrium.

SATURN RETURN

When the planet Saturn returns to the place in your chart that it occupied at the time of your birth, it has an impact. This occurs roughly every 28 years, so we can see immediately that it correlates with ages that we consider representative of different life stages and when we might anticipate change or adjustment to a different era. At 28 we can be considered at full adult maturity, probably established in our careers and relationships, maybe with children; at 56 we have reached middle age and are possibly at another of life's crossroads; and at 84, we might be considered at the full height of our wisdom, our lives almost complete. If you know the time and place of your birth date, an online Saturn return calculator can give you the exact timing.

It will also be useful to identify in which astrological sign Saturn falls in your chart, which will help you reflect on its influence, as both influences can be very illuminating about how you will experience and manage the impact of its return. Often the time leading up to a personal Saturn return is a demanding one, but the lessons learnt help inform the decisions made about how to progress your own goals. Don't fear this period, but work with its influence: knowledge is power and Saturn has a powerful energy you can harness should you choose.

THE MINOR
PLANETS

Sun sign astrology seldom makes mention of these 'minor' planets that also orbit the sun, but increasingly their subtle influence is being referenced. If you have had your birth chart done (if you know your birth time and place you can do this online) you will have access to this additional information.

Like the 10 main planets on the previous pages, these 18 minor entities will also be positioned in an astrological sign, bringing their energy to bear on these characteristics. You may, for example, have Fortuna in Leo, or Diana in Sagittarius. Look to these for their subtle influences on your birth chart and life via the sign they inhabit, all of which will serve to animate and resonate further the information you can reference on your own personal journey.

AESCULAPIA

Jupiter's grandson and a powerful healer, Aesculapia was taught by Chiron and influences us in what could be life-saving action, realised through the characteristics of the sign in which it falls in our chart.

BACCHUS

Jupiter's son, Bacchus is similarly benevolent but can sometimes lack restraint in the pursuit of pleasure. How this plays out in your chart is dependent on the sign in which it falls.

APOLLO

Jupiter's son, gifted in art, music and healing, Apollo rides the Sun across the skies. His energy literally lights up the way in which you inspire others, characterised by the sign in which it falls in your chart.

CERES

Goddess of agriculture and mother of Proserpina, Ceres is associated with the seasons and how we manage cycles of change in our lives. This energy is influenced by the sign in which it falls in our chart.

CHIRON

Teacher of the gods, Chiron knew all about healing herbs and medical practices and he lends his energy to how we tackle the impossible or the unthinkable, that which seems difficult to do.

DIANA

Jupiter's independent daughter was allowed to run free without the shackles of marriage. Where this falls in your birth chart will indicate what you are not prepared to sacrifice in order to conform.

CUPID

Son of Venus. The sign into which Cupid falls will influence how you inspire love and desire in others, not always appropriately and sometimes illogically but it can still be an enduring passion.

FORTUNA

Jupiter's daughter, who is always shown blindfolded, influences your fated role in other people's lives, how you show up for them without really understanding why, and at the right time.

HYGEIA

Daughter of Aesculapia and also associated with health, Hygeia is about how you anticipate risk and the avoidance of unwanted outcomes. The way you do this is characterised by the sign in which Hygeia falls.

MINERVA

Another of Jupiter's daughters, depicted by an owl, will show you via the energy given to a particular astrological sign in your chart how you show up at your most intelligent and smart. How you operate intellectually.

JUNO

Juno was the wife of Jupiter and her position in your chart will indicate where you will make a commitment in order to feel safe and secure. It's where you might seek protection in order to flourish.

OPS

The wife of Saturn, Ops saved the life of her son Jupiter by giving her husband a stone to eat instead of him. Her energy in our chart enables us to find positive solutions to life's demands and dilemmas.

PANACEA

Gifted with healing powers, Panacea
provides us with a remedy for all ills
and difficulties, and how this plays
out in your life will depend on the
characteristics of the astrological sign
in which her energy falls.

PSYCHE

Psyche, Venus' daughter-in-law, shows
us that part of ourselves that is easy to
love and endures through adversity,
and your soul that survives death and
flies free, like the butterfly that
depicts her.

PROSERPINA

Daughter of Ceres, abducted by Pluto,
Proserpina has to spend her life divided
between earth and the underworld and
she represents how we bridge the gulf
between different and difficult aspects
of our lives.

SALACIA

Neptune's wife, Salacia stands on
the seashore bridging land and sea,
happily bridging the two realities.
In your chart, she shows how you
can harmoniously bring two sides of
yourself together.

VESTA

VULCAN

Daughter of Saturn, Vesta's job was to protect Rome and in turn she was protected by vestal virgins. Her energy influences how we manage our relationships with competitive females and male authority figures.

Vulcan was a blacksmith who knew how to control fire and fashion metal into shape, and through the sign in which it falls in your chart will show you how you control your passion and make it work for you.

FURTHER READING

Jung's Studies in Astrology: Prophecies, Magic and the Qualities of Time,

Liz Greene, Routledge (2018)

Lunar Oracle: Harness the Power of the Moon,

Liberty Phi, OH Editions (2021)

Metaphysics of Astrology: Why Astrology Works,

Ivan Antic, Independently published (2020)

*Parkers' Astrology: The Definitive Guide to Using Astrology in Every Aspect
of Your Life*,

Julia and Derek Parker, Dorling Kindersley (2020)

USEFUL WEBSITES

Alicebellastrology.com
Astro.com
Astrology.com
Cafeastrology.com
Costarastrology.com
Jessicaadams.com

USEFUL APPS

Astro Future
Co-Star
Moon
Sanctuary
Time Nomad
Time Passages

ACKNOWLEDGEMENTS

Thanks are due to my Taurean publisher Kate Pollard for commissioning this Astrology Oracle series, to Piscean Matt Tomlinson for his careful editing, and to Evi O Studio for their beautiful design and illustrations.

ABOUT THE AUTHOR

As a sun sign Aquarius Liberty Phi loves to explore the world and has lived on three different continents, currently residing in North America. Their Gemini moon inspires them to communicate their love of astrology and other esoteric practices while Leo rising helps energise them. Their first publication, also released by OH Editions, is a box set of 36 oracle cards and accompanying guide, entitled *Lunar Oracle: Harness the Power of the Moon*.

Published in 2023 by OH Editions,
an imprint of Welbeck Non-Fiction Ltd,
part of the Welbeck Publishing Group.
Offices in London, 20 Mortimer Street, London, W1T 3JW,
and Sydney, 205 Commonwealth Street, Surry Hills, 2010.
www.welbeckpublishing.com

Design © 2023 OH Editions
Text © 2023 Liberty Phi
Illustrations © 2023 Evi O. Studio

A CIP catalogue record for this book is available from the British Library.

ISBN 978-1-91431-795-8

Publisher: Kate Pollard
Editor: Sophie Elletson
In-house editor: Matt Tomlinson
Designer: Evi O. Studio
Illustrator: Evi O. Studio
Production controller: Jess Brisley
Printed and bound by Leo Paper

10 9 8 7 6 5 4 3 2 1

ACKNOWLEDGEMENTS

Thanks are due to my Taurean publisher Kate Pollard for commissioning this Astrology Oracle series, to Piscean Matt Tomlinson for his careful editing, and to Evi O Studio for their beautiful design and illustrations.

ABOUT THE AUTHOR

As a sun sign Aquarius Liberty Phi loves to explore the world and has lived on three different continents, currently residing in North America. Their Gemini moon inspires them to communicate their love of astrology and other esoteric practices while Leo rising helps energise them. Their first publication, also released by OH Editions, is a box set of 36 oracle cards and accompanying guide, entitled *Lunar Oracle: Harness the Power of the Moon*.

Published in 2023 by OH Editions,
an imprint of Welbeck Non-Fiction Ltd,
part of the Welbeck Publishing Group.
Offices in London, 20 Mortimer Street, London, W1T 3JW,
and Sydney, 205 Commonwealth Street, Surry Hills, 2010.
www.welbeckpublishing.com

Design © 2023 OH Editions
Text © 2023 Liberty Phi
Illustrations © 2023 Evi O. Studio

A CIP catalogue record for this book is available from the British Library.

ISBN 978-1-91431-795-8

Publisher: Kate Pollard
Editor: Sophie Elleteson
In-house editor: Matt Tomlinson
Designer: Evi O. Studio
Illustrator: Evi O. Studio
Production controller: Jess Brisley
Printed and bound by Leo Paper

10 9 8 7 6 5 4 3 2 1